Computer Graphics Development With Vulkan

A Hands-On Guide to Creating Stunning Visuals and Interactive Experiences

James R. Bromley

Copyright © 2024 by James R. Bromley

No part of this publication may be reproduced, distributed, or transmitted in any form or by any means, including photocopying, recording, or other electronic or mechanical methods, without the prior written permission of the publisher, except in the case of brief quotations embodied in critical reviews and certain other noncommercial uses permitted by copyright law.

Disclaimer

This book is intended to provide general information and is not a substitute for legal, professional, or expert advice. While every effort has been made to ensure accuracy, the author and publisher assume no responsibility for errors or omissions. The views expressed in this book are solely those of the author and do not necessarily reflect the views of any organization or institution.

Contents

Introduction 5
- What is Vulkan? 5
- Why Vulkan? 6
- Setting Up the Development Environment 7
  - 1. Choose a Platform and Operating System: 7
  - 2. Install Required Tools: 8
  - 3. Configure the Development Environment: 8
- Basic Vulkan Concepts 9
  - Logical and Physical Devices 9
  - Physical Devices 9
  - Logical Devices 9
  - Memory Management 10
  - Command Buffers 11
  - Pipeline Stages 13

Fundamentals of Graphics Programming 15
- Rendering Pipeline Overview 15
- Vertex and Fragment Shaders 17
  - Vertex Shader 17
  - Fragment Shader1 18
- Uniform Buffers and Texture Samplers 20
  - Uniform Buffers 20
  - Texture Samplers 21
- Input Assembly and Geometry Shader 22
  - Input Assembly Stage 22
  - Geometry Shader 22
- Rasterization and Depth Testing 23
  - Rasterization Stage 23
  - Depth Testing 24
- Fundamentals of Graphics Programming: Blending and Color Output 24
  - Blending 25
  - Color Output 25
- Compute Shaders 26

Advanced Graphics Techniques 28
- Real-Time Lighting 28
  - Directional, Point, and Spot Lights 28
  - Directional Lights 28
  - Point Lights 28

- Spot Lights 29
- Shadow Mapping 30
- Screen-Space Ambient Occlusion (SSAO) 31
- Material Systems 32
  - Physically-Based Rendering (PBR) 32
  - Material Graphs 34
- Post-Processing Effects 35
  - Anti-Aliasing (AA) Techniques 35
  - Bloom, Depth of Field, and Motion Blur 37
  - Bloom 37
  - Depth of Field 37
  - Motion Blur 38
- Advanced Rendering Techniques 38
  - Deferred Shading 38
- Advanced Rendering Techniques: Forward+ Rendering 39
  - Volumetric Rendering 41

Interactive Techniques 43
- User Input 43
  - Keyboard and Mouse Input 43
  - Keyboard Input 43
  - Mouse Input 44
  - Gamepad Input 45
- Camera Systems 46
  - First-Person and Third-Person Cameras 46
  - First-Person Camera 46
  - Third-Person Camera 47
  - Camera Controls and Movement 48
  - Camera Movement 48
  - Camera Controls 48
- Physics Integration 50
  - Rigid Body Physics 50
  - Core Concepts 50
  - Physics Engine 50
  - Common Physics Engines 50
  - Implementing Rigid Body Physics 51
  - Advanced Techniques 51
  - Soft Body Physics 52
  - Core Concepts 52
  - Challenges in Soft Body Physics 52

    Techniques for Improving Soft Body Physics 52
    Applications of Soft Body Physics 53

Optimization and Performance **54**
  Performance Profiling Tools 54
  Shader Optimization Techniques 56
  Memory Optimization 57
  GPU Profiling and Debugging 58
  Multi-Threading and Asynchronous Operations 60
    Multi-Threading 60
    Asynchronous Operations 61

Case Studies and Projects **63**
  Creating a Simple 3D Scene 63
  Implementing a Real-Time Renderer 66
  Building a Physically-Based Renderer 68
  Developing a Game Engine 70
    Core Components of a Game Engine 70
    Implementation Challenges 71
    Popular Game Engines 71
  Optimizing a Graphics Application 72

Appendix **74**
  Vulkan API Reference 74
  Troubleshooting Tips 75
    Common Issues and Solutions 75
    Debugging Tools 76
    Best Practices 77
  Common Pitfalls and Solutions 77
    Common Pitfalls 78
    Solutions and Best Practices 79

Introduction

What is Vulkan?

Vulkan is a low-level graphics and compute API that provides direct control over a graphics card's hardware. Unlike higher-level APIs like OpenGL or DirectX, Vulkan offers a more flexible and efficient approach to graphics programming. This increased control allows developers to optimize their applications for specific hardware and achieve higher performance.

Key Features of Vulkan:

- **Low-Level Access:** Vulkan provides direct access to the GPU's hardware, enabling fine-grained control over rendering and compute operations.
- **Cross-Platform Compatibility:** Vulkan is designed to be portable across various platforms, including Windows, Linux, Android, and iOS.
- **Efficient Resource Management:** Vulkan allows for efficient management of GPU resources, such as memory and shaders, reducing overhead and improving performance.
- **Multi-Threading Support:** Vulkan supports multi-threading, enabling developers to take advantage of modern multi-core CPUs to parallelize tasks and improve performance.
- **Customizable Pipeline:** Vulkan provides a flexible pipeline that can be customized to suit specific needs, allowing for advanced rendering techniques and optimizations.

How Vulkan Works:

1. **Application:** The application creates a logical device and queues to interact with the GPU.
2. **Command Buffers:** Commands for rendering or compute operations are recorded into command buffers.
3. **Submission:** Command buffers are submitted to queues for execution by the GPU.
4. **GPU Execution:** The GPU processes the commands and performs the requested operations.
5. **Presentation:** The rendered images are presented to the display.

Why Vulkan?

While higher-level APIs like OpenGL and DirectX have long been the standard for graphics programming, Vulkan offers several advantages that make it an attractive choice for many developers:

Performance:

- **Low Overhead:** Vulkan's low-level nature reduces the overhead associated with API calls, leading to improved performance.
- **Fine-Grained Control:** Developers can optimize their applications for specific hardware and use techniques like asynchronous compute and multi-threading to maximize performance.
- **Efficient Resource Management:** Vulkan provides tools for efficient memory management and resource allocation, reducing the impact on performance.

Flexibility:

- **Customizable Pipeline:** Vulkan allows developers to create custom pipelines tailored to their specific needs, enabling advanced rendering techniques and optimizations.
- **Cross-Platform Compatibility:** Vulkan's cross-platform nature enables developers to target multiple platforms with a single codebase, reducing development time and effort.
- **Future-Proof:** Vulkan is designed to evolve with the latest hardware and software trends, ensuring that applications built with Vulkan will remain relevant for years to come.

Control:

- **Direct Hardware Access:** Vulkan provides direct access to the GPU's hardware, giving developers fine-grained control over rendering and compute operations.
- **Custom Rendering Techniques:** Vulkan enables developers to implement custom rendering techniques, such as advanced lighting and shading effects, that may not be possible with higher-level APIs.

Vulkan offers a powerful and flexible approach to graphics programming, making it an ideal choice for developers who want to create high-performance, visually stunning applications.

Setting Up the Development Environment

To start developing with Vulkan, you'll need to set up a suitable development environment. Here's a general guide:

1. Choose a Platform and Operating System:

- **Windows:** A popular choice due to its widespread use and mature development tools.

- **Linux:** Offers a variety of distributions and is often preferred by developers who value open-source software.
- **macOS:** A solid option for developers working on Apple platforms.

2. Install Required Tools:

- **Vulkan SDK:** This provides essential tools, libraries, and headers for Vulkan development. Download it from the official Vulkan website.
- **C++ Compiler and Build System:**
  - **Windows:** Visual Studio is a popular choice, providing a comprehensive IDE and compiler.
  - **Linux:** GCC or Clang are commonly used compilers, and CMake is a popular build system.
  - **macOS:** Xcode is Apple's official IDE for macOS development.
- **Text Editor or IDE:** Choose a suitable text editor or IDE for writing your Vulkan code. Popular options include Visual Studio Code, Sublime Text, and CLion.

3. Configure the Development Environment:

- **Set Up Environment Variables:** Configure environment variables to point to the Vulkan SDK and other necessary tools.
- **Create a New Project:** Set up a new project directory and create the necessary source files and build scripts.
- **Write Vulkan Code:** Start writing your Vulkan code, using the Vulkan API to create and manage graphics pipelines, render passes, and other resources.
- **Compile and Build:** Use your chosen build system (e.g., CMake) to compile and link your Vulkan code into an executable.

- **Run and Debug:** Execute your application and use debugging tools to identify and fix issues.

Note: The specific steps for setting up the development environment may vary depending on your platform and chosen tools. Refer to the official Vulkan documentation and tutorials for detailed instructions.

Remember:

- Keep your development environment up-to-date with the latest Vulkan SDK and tools.
- Refer to the Vulkan API documentation for detailed information on functions, structures, and best practices.
- Utilize online resources, forums, and communities to seek help and learn from other developers.

Basic Vulkan Concepts

Logical and Physical Devices

In Vulkan, the concept of devices is fundamental to understanding how the API interacts with the GPU hardware. There are two primary types of devices: logical devices and physical devices.

Physical Devices

A physical device represents a physical piece of GPU hardware. It could be a dedicated graphics card, an integrated GPU, or even a CPU with integrated graphics capabilities. Each physical device has its own set of features and capabilities, such as the supported shader stages, memory types, and queue families.

Logical Devices

A logical device is a software representation of a physical device. It's created by the application to interact with the physical device. A logical device provides a simplified interface to the underlying hardware and allows the application to manage resources and execute commands.

Key Points:

- **One Physical Device, Many Logical Devices:** A single physical device can have multiple logical devices associated with it. This allows for different applications to share the same physical hardware.
- **Device Features and Properties:** When creating a logical device, the application can query the physical device for its features and properties to determine what features are supported and how they should be used.
- **Queue Families:** A logical device consists of one or more queue families, each with its own set of capabilities. Queue families are used to submit commands to the GPU, such as graphics commands, compute commands, or transfer commands.

Memory Management

Memory management is a crucial aspect of Vulkan. It involves allocating, managing, and freeing memory resources on the GPU. Vulkan's memory system is more complex than that of traditional APIs, but it offers greater flexibility and control.

Memory Types: Vulkan defines different memory types, each with specific properties:

- **Host Visible:** Memory that can be accessed by both the CPU and GPU.

- **Device Local:** Memory that is only accessible by the GPU.
- **Device Local Host Cached:** Device local memory that can be cached by the CPU.

Memory Allocation: To allocate memory in Vulkan, you need to:

1. **Query Physical Device Memory Properties:** This involves querying the physical device to determine the available memory types and their properties.
2. **Allocate Memory:** Use vkAllocateMemory to allocate a block of memory of a specific size and memory type.
3. **Bind Memory:** Associate the allocated memory with a specific Vulkan object, such as a buffer or image, using vkBindBufferMemory or vkBindImageMemory.

Memory Usage and Management:

- **Staging Buffers:** Used to transfer data from the CPU to the GPU.
- **Device Local Buffers:** Used for vertex data, index data, and uniform buffers.
- **Device Local Images:** Used for textures and render targets.

Memory Management Best Practices:

- **Minimize Memory Transfers:** Reduce the amount of data transferred between the CPU and GPU by using staging buffers efficiently.
- **Optimize Memory Allocations:** Allocate memory in larger chunks to reduce fragmentation and improve performance.
- **Use Memory Barriers:** Ensure proper synchronization between different memory operations.

Command Buffers

Command buffers are the primary mechanism for recording commands in Vulkan. They store a sequence of drawing commands, compute commands, or transfer commands that will be executed by the GPU. By using command buffers, developers can efficiently batch together multiple operations and improve performance.

Recording Commands: To record commands into a command buffer, you need to:

1. **Begin Recording:** Start a recording session using vkBeginCommandBuffer.
2. **Record Commands:** Use various Vulkan functions to record commands, such as:
   - vkCmdDraw for drawing primitives
   - vkCmdDrawIndexed for drawing indexed primitives
   - vkCmdDispatchCompute for executing compute shaders
   - vkCmdCopyBuffer for copying data between buffers
   - vkCmdPipelineBarrier for synchronizing access to resources
3. **End Recording:** Finish the recording session using vkEndCommandBuffer.

Submitting Command Buffers: Once a command buffer is recorded, it can be submitted to a queue for execution. The queue will process the commands and execute them on the GPU. To submit a command buffer, you need to:

1. **Create a Submit Info Structure:** Create a VkSubmitInfo structure to specify the command buffers to be submitted, wait semaphores, and signal semaphores.
2. **Submit to Queue:** Use vkQueueSubmit to submit the command buffer to the queue.

Command Buffer Levels: Vulkan supports two levels of command buffers:

- **Primary Command Buffers:** Can be submitted directly to a queue.
- **Secondary Command Buffers:** Can only be called from within a primary command buffer.

Pipeline Stages

The Vulkan pipeline is a series of processing stages that a graphics card goes through to render a scene. Each stage takes input, processes it, and passes the result to the next stage. Understanding these stages is essential for optimizing graphics performance and creating visually appealing graphics.

The main pipeline stages in Vulkan are:

1. **Vertex Input Assembly:**
   - Fetches vertex data from vertex buffers.
   - Assembles vertices into primitives (points, lines, or triangles).
2. **Vertex Shader:**
   - Processes individual vertices, transforming their positions, colors, and texture coordinates.
   - Can also calculate lighting and other effects.
3. **Tessellation Control and Evaluation Shaders:**
   - Optional stages used for tessellation, which subdivides primitives into smaller ones for more detailed rendering.
4. **Geometry Shader:**
   - Optional stage that can modify or generate new primitives.

5. **Rasterization:**
   - Converts primitives into fragments, which are small colored pieces that make up the final image.
6. **Fragment Shader:**
   - Processes individual fragments, calculating their final color and depth values.
7. **Early Fragment Tests:**
   - Performs early depth and stencil tests to discard fragments that are not visible.
8. **Late Fragment Tests and Blending:**
   - Performs depth and stencil tests, blending, and color output.

Fundamentals of Graphics Programming

Rendering Pipeline Overview

The rendering pipeline is a series of stages that a graphics card goes through to render a 3D scene. It takes input data, such as vertex and texture information, and processes it to produce a 2D image on the screen.

The primary stages of the rendering pipeline are:

1. **Vertex Shader:**
    - Processes individual vertices, transforming their positions, colors, and texture coordinates.
    - Can also calculate lighting and other effects.
2. **Tessellation Control and Evaluation Shaders:**
    - Optional stages used for tessellation, which subdivides primitives into smaller ones for more detailed rendering.
3. **Geometry Shader:**
    - Optional stage that can modify or generate new primitives.
4. **Rasterization:**
    - Converts primitives (triangles) into fragments, which are small colored pieces that make up the final image.
5. **Fragment Shader:**
    - Processes individual fragments, calculating their final color and depth values.
6. **Early Fragment Tests:**

- Performs early depth and stencil tests to discard fragments that are not visible.

7. **Late Fragment Tests and Blending:**
   - Performs depth and stencil tests, blending, and color output.

Key Concepts:

- **Vertex Shader:**
  - Takes input vertex data and transforms it into clip space coordinates.
  - Calculates per-vertex lighting and other effects.
  - Outputs transformed vertex data, including position, color, texture coordinates, and normal vectors.

- **Tessellation Shaders:**
  - Used for tessellation, which subdivides primitives into smaller ones.
  - Tessellation control shader determines the level of tessellation.
  - Tessellation evaluation shader generates new vertices for the subdivided primitives.

- **Geometry Shader:**
  - Can emit new primitives or modify existing ones.
  - Useful for procedural geometry generation, instancing, and other advanced techniques.

- **Rasterization:**
  - Converts primitives into fragments.
  - Calculates the depth value for each fragment.
  - Performs depth testing to determine which fragments are visible.

- **Fragment Shader:**
  - Calculates the final color of each fragment.

- Can perform complex lighting, texturing, and post-processing effects.
- Outputs the final color and depth values.

Vertex and Fragment Shaders

Vertex and fragment shaders are two of the most important stages in the graphics pipeline. They allow developers to manipulate and transform the geometry and appearance of 3D models.

Vertex Shader

The vertex shader processes individual vertices of a 3D model. Its primary tasks include:

- **Transforming Vertices:** The vertex shader transforms the vertex positions from model space to clip space. This involves applying model, view, and projection matrices.
- **Calculating Per-Vertex Attributes:** The vertex shader can calculate per-vertex attributes like lighting, texture coordinates, and normal vectors.
- **Outputting Vertex Data:** The vertex shader outputs the transformed vertex data, including the position, color, texture coordinates, and other attributes.

Example Vertex Shader:

OpenGL Shading Language

```
#version 450

layout (location = 0) in vec3 aPos;
layout (location = 1) in vec3 aNormal;
```

```glsl
layout (location = 2) in vec2 aTexCoords;

out vec3 FragPos;
out vec3 Normal;
out vec2 TexCoords;

uniform mat4 model;
uniform mat4 view;
uniform mat4 projection;

void main()
{
    FragPos = vec3(model * vec4(aPos, 1.0));
    Normal = mat3(transpose(inverse(model))) * aNormal;
    TexCoords = aTexCoords;

    gl_Position = projection * view * model * vec4(aPos, 1.0);
}
```

Fragment Shader[1]

The fragment shader processes individual fragments, which are small colored pieces that make up the final image. Its primary tasks include:

- **Calculating Pixel Color:** The fragment shader calculates the final color of each pixel based on various factors like lighting, texturing, and material properties.
- **Applying Post-Processing Effects:** The fragment shader can apply post-processing effects like bloom, depth of field, and motion blur.

- **Outputting Pixel Color:** The fragment shader outputs the final color of the pixel.

Example Fragment Shader:

OpenGL Shading Language

```glsl
#version 450

in vec3 FragPos;
in vec3 Normal;
in vec2 TexCoords;

out vec4 FragColor;

uniform sampler2D texture1;
uniform vec3 lightPos;
uniform vec3 lightColor;

void main()
{
    // Calculate lighting
    vec3 lightDir = normalize(lightPos - FragPos);
    float diff = max(dot(Normal, lightDir), 0.0);
    vec3 diffuse = diff * lightColor;

    // Texture the surface
    vec4 texColor = texture(texture1, TexCoords);

    // Combine lighting and texture
    FragColor = vec4(diffuse * texColor.rgb, 1.0);
}
```

Uniform Buffers and Texture Samplers

Uniform buffers and texture samplers are essential components of modern graphics programming, allowing for dynamic data and texture-based rendering.

Uniform Buffers

Uniform buffers are used to pass data from the CPU to the GPU. This data can be used to control various aspects of the rendering pipeline, such as:

- **Material properties:** Color, shininess, and texture information.
- **Camera transformations:** Model, view, and projection matrices.
- **Lighting parameters:** Light positions, colors, and intensities.

Uniform buffers are updated on the CPU and then sent to the GPU. The GPU can then access this data in its shaders to perform calculations and rendering.

Example Usage in a Vertex Shader:

OpenGL Shading Language

```glsl
#version 450

layout (location = 0) in vec3 aPos;
layout (location = 1) in vec2 aTexCoords;

out vec2 TexCoords;
```

```glsl
uniform UBO {
   mat4 model;
   mat4 view;
   mat4 projection;
} ubo;

void main() {
   TexCoords = aTexCoords;
      gl_Position = ubo.projection * ubo.view * ubo.model * vec4(aPos, 1.0);
}
```

Texture Samplers

Texture samplers allow you to access and sample textures from within shaders. Textures are 2D or 3D arrays of color values that can be used to add detail and realism to 3D scenes.

Example Usage in a Fragment Shader:

OpenGL Shading Language

```glsl
#version 450

in vec2 TexCoords;

out vec4 FragColor;

uniform sampler2D texture1;

void main() {
   FragColor = texture(texture1, TexCoords);
```

}

Input Assembly and Geometry Shader

Input Assembly Stage

The input assembly stage takes vertex data from vertex buffers and assembles them into primitives, such as points, lines, or triangles. The vertex shader processes each vertex individually, and the input assembly stage groups these vertices into primitives.

The input assembly stage uses an index buffer to specify the order in which vertices should be assembled. This allows for efficient rendering of complex models with shared vertices.

Geometry Shader

The geometry shader is an optional stage that can be used to manipulate primitives. It takes as input primitives (points, lines, or triangles) and can output new primitives of any type.

Some common use cases for geometry shaders include:

- **Tessellation:** Subdividing primitives into smaller ones to increase detail.
- **Instancing:** Creating multiple instances of a primitive, each with slightly different transformations.
- **Procedural geometry generation:** Generating complex geometry on the fly.

Example Geometry Shader:

OpenGL Shading Language

```glsl
#version 450

layout (triangles) in;
layout (triangle_strip, max_vertices = 3) out;

in vec3 in_Position[];

out vec3 out_Position[];

void main() {
   // Emit the first triangle
   gl_Position = gl_in[0].gl_Position;
   EmitVertex();
   gl_Position = gl_in[1].gl_Position;
   EmitVertex();
   gl_Position = gl_in[2].gl_Position;
   EmitVertex();
   EndPrimitive();

   // Emit the second triangle
   // ...
}
```

Rasterization and Depth Testing

Rasterization Stage

The rasterization stage is responsible for converting geometric primitives (triangles) into fragments, which are small colored pieces that make up the final image. This process involves:

1. **Triangle Rasterization:**
   - The rasterizer determines which pixels are covered by each triangle.
   - For each covered pixel, the rasterizer interpolates the vertex attributes (color, texture coordinates, depth) to calculate the corresponding values for the fragment.
2. **Fragment Generation:**
   - For each covered pixel, a fragment is generated with the interpolated attributes.

Depth Testing

Depth testing is a technique used to determine which fragments are visible. It involves comparing the depth value of each fragment to the depth value of the fragment that is currently stored in the depth buffer at the same pixel location.

The depth buffer is a buffer that stores the depth values of each pixel. When a fragment is generated, its depth value is compared to the depth value in the depth buffer. If the new fragment is closer to the camera, it overwrites the existing fragment. Otherwise, the existing fragment is kept.

Depth testing helps to prevent overlapping objects from incorrectly obscuring each other. It is essential for creating realistic 3D scenes.

Fundamentals of Graphics Programming: Blending and Color Output

Blending

Blending is a technique used to combine the color of a new fragment with the color of the existing fragment in the framebuffer. This is often used to achieve transparency effects, such as alpha blending, or to combine multiple rendering passes.

Alpha Blending: Alpha blending is a common blending technique used to blend transparent objects with the background. It involves multiplying the color of the new fragment by its alpha value and adding it to the color of the existing fragment, weighted by its alpha value.

Other Blending Techniques:

- **Additive Blending:** Adds the colors of the new and existing fragments.
- **Subtractive Blending:** Subtracts the colors of the new and existing fragments.
- **Multiplicative Blending:** Multiplies the colors of the new and existing fragments.

Color Output

The final stage of the rendering pipeline is color output. The color of each fragment is written to the framebuffer, which is a buffer that stores the final image. The framebuffer is then displayed on the screen.

Color Space: The color of a fragment is typically represented in a specific color space, such as sRGB or linear RGB. The choice of color space can affect the appearance of the final image.

Gamma Correction: Gamma correction is a technique used to compensate for the non-linear response of displays. It ensures that the perceived brightness of colors is accurate.

Compute Shaders

Compute shaders are a powerful tool for general-purpose computing on the GPU. Unlike other shader stages that are primarily used for rendering graphics, compute shaders can be used to perform a wide range of tasks, including:

- **Physics simulations:** Simulating physical phenomena like fluid dynamics, cloth simulation, and rigid body dynamics.
- **Image processing:** Applying filters, effects, and transformations to images.
- **Ray tracing:** Simulating the path of light rays to create realistic lighting and reflections.
- **Artificial intelligence:** Training and running machine learning models.

How Compute Shaders Work:

1. **Dispatch:** The application dispatches a number of work groups to the GPU.
2. **Work Group Execution:** Each work group consists of a number of work items.
3. **Kernel Execution:** The compute shader kernel is executed for each work item within a work group.

Example Compute Shader:

OpenGL Shading Language

```glsl
#version 450

layout (local_size_x = 32, local_size_y = 32, local_size_z = 1) in;

uniform float deltaTime;
uniform sampler2D inputImage;
uniform image2D outputImage;

void main() {
    ivec2 pixelCoords = ivec2(gl_GlobalInvocationID.xy);
    vec4 inputColor = texelFetch(inputImage, pixelCoords, 0);

    // Apply a simple blur effect
    vec4 blurredColor = vec4(0.0);
    for (int x = -1; x <= 1; ++x) {
        for (int y = -1; y <= 1; ++y) {
            ivec2 neighborCoords = pixelCoords + ivec2(x, y);
            blurredColor += texelFetch(inputImage, neighborCoords, 0);
        }
    }
    blurredColor /= 9.0;

    imageStore(outputImage, pixelCoords, blurredColor);
}
```

Advanced Graphics Techniques

Real-Time Lighting

Directional, Point, and Spot Lights

Real-time lighting is a critical component of modern 3D graphics, allowing for dynamic and realistic illumination of scenes. Three fundamental types of lights commonly used in real-time rendering are directional, point, and spot lights.

Directional Lights

A directional light simulates a light source that is infinitely far away, such as the sun. Its rays are parallel, and its intensity is constant across the scene.

Key characteristics of directional lights:

- **Direction:** A vector specifying the direction of the light's rays.
- **Color:** The color of the light.
- **Intensity:** The strength of the light.

Point Lights

A point light simulates a light source that emits light uniformly in all directions.

Key characteristics of point lights:

- **Position:** The position of the light source in 3D space.
- **Color:** The color of the light.

- **Intensity:** The strength of the light.
- **Attenuation:** A factor that determines how the light's intensity decreases with distance.

Spot Lights

A spot light simulates a light source that emits light within a cone-shaped region. It's often used to simulate spotlights, flashlights, and other focused light sources.

Key characteristics of spot lights:

- **Position:** The position of the light source in 3D space.
- **Direction:** The direction of the light's cone.
- **Color:** The color of the light.
- **Intensity:** The strength of the light.
- **Inner and Outer Cone Angles:** These angles define the shape of the light cone.
- **Attenuation:** A factor that determines how the light's intensity decreases with distance and angle.

Implementation Techniques:

- **Per-Pixel Lighting:** The lighting calculations are performed for each pixel in the fragment shader. This allows for more detailed and realistic lighting, but can be computationally expensive.
- **Per-Vertex Lighting:** The lighting calculations are performed for each vertex in the vertex shader. This is less accurate than per-pixel lighting, but it can be more efficient.
- **Lightmaps:** Pre-calculated lighting information is stored in textures and applied to surfaces during rendering. This can be used to reduce the computational cost of real-time lighting.

Shadow Mapping

Shadow mapping is a technique used to create realistic shadows in real-time 3D graphics. It involves rendering the scene from the light's point of view to generate a depth map, which is then used to determine which parts of the scene are in shadow.

How Shadow Mapping Works:

1. **Depth Map Generation:**
   - The scene is rendered from the light's point of view, capturing the depth information of each pixel.
   - The depth information is stored in a texture, known as the depth map.
2. **Shadow Rendering:**
   - The scene is rendered from the camera's point of view.
   - For each fragment, the position of the fragment in light space is calculated.
   - The depth value of the fragment in light space is compared to the corresponding depth value in the depth map.
   - If the fragment is farther away from the light source than the depth value in the depth map, it is in shadow.

Challenges and Optimizations:

- **Shadow Mapping Artifacts:** Shadow mapping can suffer from artifacts like shadow acne and peter panning. These artifacts can be mitigated using techniques like shadow bias and filtering.
- **Performance Cost:** Generating and sampling depth maps can be computationally expensive. To improve performance, techniques like cascaded shadow maps and variance shadow maps can be used.

Additional Techniques:

- **Shadow Volumes:** Another technique for creating shadows, which involves creating volumes around objects that cast shadows.
- **Screen Space Ambient Occlusion (SSAO):** A technique for simulating ambient occlusion, which is the darkening of surfaces due to the occlusion of ambient light.

Screen-Space Ambient Occlusion (SSAO)

Screen-Space Ambient Occlusion (SSAO) is a post-processing technique used to simulate the darkening of surfaces due to ambient light being occluded by nearby surfaces. It's a relatively inexpensive technique that can significantly improve the realism of a scene.

How SSAO Works:

1. **Depth Buffer:** The depth buffer is used to store the depth information of the scene.
2. **Kernel:** A kernel is used to sample the depth values of nearby pixels.
3. **Occlusion Calculation:** For each pixel, the depth values of nearby pixels are compared to the current pixel's depth. If the nearby pixels are closer, it indicates occlusion.
4. **Occlusion Factor:** An occlusion factor is calculated based on the number of occluded samples.
5. **Color Adjustment:** The final color of the pixel is adjusted by multiplying it with the occlusion factor.

Key Techniques and Considerations:

- **Kernel Design:** The choice of kernel size and shape can significantly impact the quality and performance of SSAO.

- **Noise:** To avoid banding artifacts, noise is often added to the sampling process.
- **Performance Optimization:** Techniques like hardware acceleration and asynchronous computation can be used to improve performance.
- **Quality vs. Performance:** There is a trade-off between the quality of SSAO and its performance cost.

Additional Techniques:

- **Horizon-Based Ambient Occlusion (HBAO):** A more advanced technique that takes into account the horizon of the scene to improve accuracy.
- **Screen-Space Reflective Shadow Maps (SSR):** A technique that combines SSAO with reflections to create more realistic lighting.

Material Systems

Physically-Based Rendering (PBR)

Physically-Based Rendering (PBR) is a rendering technique that aims to simulate the real-world behavior of light interacting with materials. It provides a more realistic and predictable appearance for 3D objects.

Core Concepts of PBR:

1. **Microfacet Theory:**
    - Models the surface of a material as a collection of tiny microfacets, each with its own orientation.

- The distribution of microfacet orientations determines the material's roughness.
2. **Energy Conservation:**
   - Ensures that the amount of light reflected from a surface is equal to the amount of light incident on the surface.
   - This prevents unrealistic, overly bright materials.
3. **Specular and Diffuse Reflections:**
   - **Specular Reflection:** The mirror-like reflection of light from a surface.
   - **Diffuse Reflection:** The scattering of light in all directions from a surface.

Key PBR Material Properties:

- **Albedo:** The base color of the material.
- **Metallic:** Determines how metallic the material is.
- **Roughness:** Controls the roughness of the surface, affecting the sharpness of specular reflections.
- **Specular:** Controls the intensity of specular reflections.

PBR Rendering Equation:

The rendering equation is a mathematical model that describes how light interacts with a surface. In PBR, the rendering equation is simplified and approximated to achieve real-time performance.

Implementation Techniques:

- **Standard PBR Workflow:**
  - Create a PBR material with albedo, metallic, roughness, and specular properties.
  - Use a physically-based shading model, such as the Physically Based Rendering (PBR) model, to calculate the lighting and shading of the material.

- **Texture Maps:**
    - Use texture maps to provide detailed information about the material's properties, such as albedo, metallic, roughness, and normal maps.

Material Graphs

Material graphs are a visual programming system used to create and customize materials in real-time. They provide a node-based interface where nodes represent different operations on materials, and edges connect these nodes to define the flow of data.

Key Components of Material Graphs:

- **Nodes:**
    - **Input Nodes:** Provide input values, such as textures, colors, and numbers.
    - **Operation Nodes:** Perform mathematical operations, color manipulations, and texture sampling.
    - **Output Nodes:** Output the final material properties.
- **Edges:** Connect nodes to define the flow of data between them.

Benefits of Material Graphs:

- **Visual and Intuitive:** Material graphs provide a visual representation of the material creation process, making it easier to understand and modify.
- **Flexibility:** Users can create complex materials by combining various nodes and operations.
- **Real-time Editing:** Changes to the material graph are reflected immediately in the scene, allowing for rapid iteration and experimentation.

- **Shared Materials:** Material graphs can be shared and reused across different projects.

Common Use Cases:

- **Creating Custom Materials:** Users can create unique materials with specific properties, such as metallic, dielectric, or translucent materials.
- **Procedural Textures:** Material graphs can be used to generate procedural textures, such as noise, marble, and wood.
- **Material Variants:** By creating variations of a base material, developers can reduce the number of unique materials in a project.

Post-Processing Effects

Anti-Aliasing (AA) Techniques

Anti-aliasing (AA) is a technique used to reduce the jagged edges, or aliasing, that can occur when rendering 3D graphics. By smoothing out these edges, AA can significantly improve the visual quality of a scene.

Common Anti-Aliasing Techniques:

1. **Multi-Sampling Anti-Aliasing (MSAA):**
   - Renders the scene multiple times from slightly different viewpoints.
   - Samples multiple color values for each pixel and averages them to reduce aliasing.

- Effective for reducing jagged edges on geometry, but can be computationally expensive.

2. **Super-Sampling Anti-Aliasing (SSAA):**
   - Renders the scene at a higher resolution than the display.
   - Downsamples the high-resolution image to the display resolution, reducing aliasing.
   - Very effective but computationally expensive.

3. **Fast Approximate Anti-Aliasing (FXAA):**
   - A post-processing technique that analyzes the image and applies a filter to smooth out edges.
   - Less computationally expensive than MSAA and SSAA, but can introduce some artifacts.

4. **Sub-Pixel Morphological Anti-Aliasing (SMAA):**
   - A more advanced technique that analyzes the edges in the image and applies a customized filter to each edge.
   - Provides better quality than FXAA, but can be more computationally expensive.

5. **Temporal Anti-Aliasing (TAA):**
   - Combines multiple frames of the scene to reduce temporal aliasing, which occurs when objects move quickly.
   - Can produce smoother motion and reduce flickering, but can introduce ghosting artifacts.

Choosing the Right Technique:

The choice of anti-aliasing technique depends on factors such as:

- **Target Platform:** The capabilities of the target platform, including the GPU and CPU.
- **Desired Image Quality:** The level of anti-aliasing required for the specific application.

- **Performance Budget:** The available computational resources.

Bloom, Depth of Field, and Motion Blur

Post-processing effects are techniques applied to an image after it has been rendered to enhance its visual appeal. Some common post-processing effects include bloom, depth of field, and motion blur.

Bloom

Bloom is a technique that simulates the effect of light bleeding or blooming around bright objects. It can add a sense of realism and atmosphere to a scene.

How Bloom Works:

1. **Bright Pass:** A bright pass filter is applied to the image to identify bright areas.
2. **Blur:** The bright areas are blurred multiple times to create a soft glow.
3. **Blending:** The blurred image is blended with the original image to produce the final result.

Depth of Field

Depth of field simulates the way a camera lens focuses on a specific distance, blurring objects in the foreground and background.

How Depth of Field Works:

1. **Depth Buffer:** The depth buffer is used to determine the distance of each pixel from the camera.

2. **Blur Kernel:** A blur kernel is applied to pixels that are out of focus, based on their distance from the focus plane.
3. **Blending:** The blurred pixels are blended with the in-focus pixels to create the final image.

Motion Blur

Motion blur simulates the effect of camera motion or object motion on the image. It can add a sense of speed and dynamism to a scene.

How Motion Blur Works:

1. **Motion Vectors:** Motion vectors are calculated for each pixel to determine the direction and magnitude of motion.
2. **Blur Kernel:** A blur kernel is applied to each pixel, weighted by the motion vector.
3. **Blending:** The blurred pixels are blended with the original pixels to create the final image.

Advanced Rendering Techniques

Deferred Shading

Deferred shading is a rendering technique that separates the geometry and lighting passes, improving performance and enabling more complex lighting effects.

Traditional Forward Rendering:

In traditional forward rendering, for each pixel, the scene is rendered multiple times, once for each light source. This can be inefficient, especially in scenes with many light sources.

Deferred Shading Pipeline:

1. **Geometry Pass:**
   - Renders the geometry of the scene, storing information about the position, normal, albedo, and other material properties for each pixel in G-buffers.
2. **Lighting Pass:**
   - For each pixel, the lighting calculations are performed using the information stored in the G-buffers.
   - This allows for efficient lighting calculations, as the geometry only needs to be processed once.

Advantages of Deferred Shading:

- **Efficient Lighting:** By separating the geometry and lighting passes, deferred shading allows for efficient lighting calculations, especially in scenes with many light sources.
- **Advanced Lighting Effects:** Deferred shading enables more complex lighting effects, such as advanced global illumination techniques.
- **Reduced Overdraw:** By rendering the geometry only once, deferred shading can reduce overdraw, which occurs when multiple objects overlap and are rendered multiple times.

Disadvantages of Deferred Shading:

- **Increased Memory Usage:** Deferred shading requires additional memory to store the G-buffers.
- **Complexity:** Implementing deferred shading can be more complex than forward rendering.

Advanced Rendering Techniques: Forward+ Rendering

Forward+ rendering is a hybrid rendering technique that combines the best aspects of forward rendering and deferred shading. It aims to balance performance and flexibility by using a combination of techniques.

How Forward+ Rendering Works:

1. **Geometry Pass:**
   - Renders the geometry of the scene, storing information about the position, normal, albedo, and other material properties for each pixel.
2. **Lighting Pass:**
   - For each pixel, the lighting calculations are performed using a combination of forward and deferred techniques.
   - For simple lighting, such as directional lights, the calculations can be performed directly in the pixel shader.
   - For more complex lighting, such as point lights and spot lights, deferred shading techniques can be used to reduce the number of lighting calculations.

Advantages of Forward+ Rendering:

- **Balance of Performance and Flexibility:** Forward+ rendering provides a good balance between performance and flexibility.
- **Reduced Memory Usage:** Compared to deferred shading, forward+ rendering requires less memory.
- **Simpler Implementation:** Forward+ rendering can be easier to implement than deferred shading.

Disadvantages of Forward+ Rendering:

- **Limited Scalability:** Forward+ rendering may not scale as well as deferred shading for complex scenes with many light sources.

- **Performance Overhead:** The additional overhead of combining forward and deferred techniques can impact performance.

Volumetric Rendering

Volumetric rendering is a technique for rendering 3D objects that are defined by a volume of space, rather than by a surface. This allows for the creation of realistic effects like fog, smoke, and fire.

How Volumetric Rendering Works:

1. **Volume Data:** The 3D volume is represented by a 3D texture, where each voxel (volume pixel) stores information about the material properties, such as density, color, and opacity.
2. **Ray Marching:** A ray is cast from the camera through the volume.
3. **Density Sampling:** The ray samples the density of the volume at each step.
4. **Opacity Accumulation:** The opacity of the ray is accumulated as it travels through the volume.
5. **Color Calculation:** The color of the ray is calculated based on the density, color, and lighting conditions at each step.
6. **Early Termination:** If the opacity of the ray reaches a certain threshold, the ray can be terminated early to improve performance.

Challenges and Optimizations:

- **Computational Cost:** Volumetric rendering can be computationally expensive, especially for large volumes and high-resolution textures.
- **Memory Usage:** Storing large volumes of data can consume significant memory.

- **Aliasing Artifacts:** Aliasing artifacts can occur when sampling the volume.

Techniques for Optimization:

- **Hierarchical Volume Data Structures:** Using hierarchical data structures, such as octrees or kd-trees, can reduce the number of voxels that need to be processed.
- **Precomputed Radiance Transfer (PRT):** Pre-computing the lighting and scattering of light within the volume can reduce the computational cost at runtime.
- **GPU Acceleration:** Leveraging the power of GPUs can significantly accelerate volumetric rendering.

Interactive Techniques

User Input

Keyboard and Mouse Input

User input is a crucial aspect of interactive applications. Keyboard and mouse input are fundamental methods for users to interact with 3D scenes.

Keyboard Input

Keyboard input is typically handled by polling or event-driven mechanisms.

Polling:

- Continuously checks the keyboard state to see if any keys are pressed.
- Can be less efficient, especially for high-frequency input.

Event-Driven:

- Relies on the operating system to generate events when keys are pressed or released.
- More efficient and responsive.

Key Considerations:

- **Key Codes:** Different operating systems use different key codes to represent keys. It's important to use a platform-independent way to handle key codes.

- **Key Repeat:** To prevent excessive key repetition, you can implement a debouncing mechanism.
- **Input Mapping:** Mapping keyboard keys to specific actions in the game or application.

Mouse Input

Mouse input provides information about the position of the mouse cursor and button presses.

Mouse Position:

- The position of the mouse cursor is typically represented by x and y coordinates relative to the screen or window.
- This information can be used to control camera movement, select objects, or perform other actions.

Mouse Buttons:

- Mouse buttons (left, right, and middle) can be used to trigger actions or modify input.
- For example, the left mouse button can be used to select objects, while the right mouse button can be used to activate a context menu.

Mouse Wheel:

- The mouse wheel can be used to scroll through menus, zoom in and out, or control other functions.

Key Considerations:

- **Mouse Sensitivity:** The sensitivity of the mouse can affect how quickly the cursor moves.
- **Cursor Visibility:** You can control the visibility of the mouse cursor to provide a more immersive experience.

- **Mouse Locking:** Locking the mouse cursor to the screen can be useful for first-person games.

Gamepad Input

Gamepads offer a more intuitive and immersive way to interact with games and other interactive applications. They provide a variety of input options, including buttons, analog sticks, and triggers.

Gamepad Input Handling:

1. **Gamepad Detection:**
   - Detect connected gamepads using platform-specific APIs or libraries.
2. **Input Reading:**
   - Read the state of buttons, analog sticks, and triggers.
   - This can be done through polling or event-driven mechanisms.
3. **Input Mapping:**
   - Map gamepad inputs to specific actions in the game or application.
   - This can be done using a configuration file or a user interface.

Key Considerations:

- **Input Latency:** Minimize input latency to ensure a responsive experience.
- **Dead Zones:** Implement dead zones for analog sticks to reduce accidental input.
- **Vibration Feedback:** Use vibration feedback to enhance the gaming experience.

- **Custom Input Mappings:** Allow users to customize input mappings to suit their preferences.

Popular Gamepad APIs:

- **XInput:** Microsoft's API for Xbox controllers.
- **DirectInput:** Microsoft's API for a wide range of gamepads.
- **SDL Game Controller:** A cross-platform library for handling gamepads.

Camera Systems

First-Person and Third-Person Cameras

Camera systems are essential for creating immersive and engaging 3D experiences. Two common types of cameras used in games and simulations are first-person and third-person cameras.

First-Person Camera

A first-person camera simulates the view from the eyes of a character, providing a subjective perspective. It's commonly used in first-person shooter games and virtual reality experiences.

Key Components:

- **Position:** The camera's position is typically tied to the player character's position.
- **Rotation:** The camera's rotation is controlled by the player's input, such as mouse movement or keyboard keys.
- **Field of View:** The field of view determines the visible area of the scene.

Implementation:

1. **Update Position:** Update the camera's position based on player movement and input.
2. **Update Rotation:** Update the camera's rotation based on player input.
3. **Calculate View Matrix:** Create a view matrix that transforms world-space coordinates to camera-space coordinates.
4. **Apply View Matrix:** Apply the view matrix to the vertices of objects in the scene to project them onto the screen.

Third-Person Camera

A third-person camera provides a view of the scene from a distance, typically following a character or object. It's commonly used in action-adventure games and role-playing games.

Key Components:

- **Position:** The camera's position is calculated based on the target object's position and the desired camera distance.
- **Rotation:** The camera's rotation can be controlled by the player or automatically adjusted to maintain a good view of the target.
- **Field of View:** The field of view determines the visible area of the scene.

Implementation:

1. **Calculate Camera Position:** Calculate the camera's position based on the target object's position and the desired distance and angle.
2. **Calculate Camera Rotation:** Calculate the camera's rotation to face the target object.

3. **Create View Matrix:** Create a view matrix that transforms world-space coordinates to camera-space coordinates.
4. **Apply View Matrix:** Apply the view matrix to the vertices of objects in the scene to project them onto the screen.

Camera Controls and Movement

Effective camera controls are essential for creating immersive and intuitive user experiences. By understanding the principles of camera movement and control, developers can create seamless and enjoyable gameplay experiences.

Camera Movement

Basic Movement:

- **Forward/Backward:** Move the camera forward or backward along its local Z-axis.
- **Strafe Left/Right:** Move the camera left or right along its local X-axis.
- **Look Up/Down:** Rotate the camera around its local X-axis.
- **Look Left/Right:** Rotate the camera around its local Y-axis.

Advanced Movement:

- **Free-Look:** Allow the player to look around independently of movement direction.
- **Smooth Camera Movement:** Use interpolation or easing functions to create smooth camera transitions.
- **Camera Bobbing and Sway:** Simulate camera movement due to character movement and terrain.
- **Dynamic Camera:** Adjust camera position and orientation based on gameplay events or character actions.

Camera Controls

Mouse and Keyboard:

- **Mouse Movement:** Use mouse movement to control camera rotation.
- **WASD Keys:** Use WASD keys to control forward/backward and strafe left/right movement.
- **QE Keys:** Use QE keys to control up/down movement.

Gamepad:

- **Left Analog Stick:** Control camera rotation.
- **Right Analog Stick:** Control camera movement.
- **D-Pad:** Control directional movement.
- **Triggers:** Control acceleration or deceleration.

Touchscreen:

- **Swipe Gestures:** Use swipe gestures to control camera rotation and movement.
- **Pinch Gestures:** Use pinch gestures to zoom in and out.
- **Tap Gestures:** Use tap gestures to select objects or trigger actions.

Key Considerations:

- **Camera Sensitivity:** Adjust camera sensitivity to balance responsiveness and precision.
- **Camera Smoothing:** Use smoothing techniques to reduce camera jitter and improve visual quality.
- **Camera Limits:** Implement limits to prevent the camera from moving outside the desired boundaries.
- **Player Comfort:** Consider the player's comfort and avoid excessive camera motion or abrupt changes.

Physics Integration

Rigid Body Physics

Rigid body physics is a fundamental concept in game development, used to simulate the physical behavior of solid objects in a virtual environment. By understanding the principles of rigid body physics, developers can create realistic and dynamic interactions between objects.

Core Concepts

- **Rigid Body:** A solid object that maintains its shape and size, regardless of the forces acting upon it.
- **Mass:** A measure of an object's resistance to acceleration.
- **Inertia Tensor:** A matrix that describes an object's resistance to rotational acceleration.
- **Force:** A push or pull that can change an object's motion.
- **Torque:** A rotational force that can change an object's angular momentum.

Physics Engine

A physics engine is a software system that simulates the physical behavior of objects in a virtual environment. It typically handles:

- **Collision Detection:** Detecting when objects collide with each other.
- **Collision Response:** Calculating the response to collisions, such as bouncing, sliding, or sticking.
- **Integration:** Integrating the equations of motion to update the positions and velocities of objects over time.

Common Physics Engines

- **PhysX:** A powerful and widely used physics engine developed by NVIDIA.
- **Bullet:** An open-source physics engine known for its stability and performance.
- **Box2D:** A 2D physics engine optimized for games.
- **Havok:** A commercial physics engine used in many AAA games.

Implementing Rigid Body Physics

1. **Create Rigid Bodies:** Define the physical properties of objects, such as mass, inertia tensor, and collision shape.
2. **Apply Forces and Torques:** Apply forces and torques to objects to simulate real-world interactions.
3. **Collision Detection:** Use algorithms like swept AABB or GJK to detect collisions between objects.
4. **Collision Response:** Calculate the response to collisions, taking into account factors like restitution, friction, and impulse.
5. **Integration:** Use numerical integration methods, such as Euler integration or Verlet integration, to update the positions and velocities of objects over time.

Advanced Techniques

- **Constraint-Based Dynamics:** Use constraints to enforce specific relationships between objects, such as joints and hinges.
- **Character Controllers:** Create realistic character movement by combining rigid body physics with kinematic control.
- **Cloth Simulation:** Simulate the behavior of cloth and other flexible materials.

- **Fluid Dynamics:** Simulate the behavior of fluids, such as water and smoke.

Soft Body Physics

Soft body physics is a branch of physics simulation that deals with the behavior of deformable objects, such as cloth, hair, and flesh. It's a more complex topic than rigid body physics, as it requires simulating the continuous deformation of objects.

Core Concepts

- **Mass-Spring System:** A common approach to soft body simulation, where objects are represented as a network of interconnected mass points and springs.
- **Finite Element Method (FEM):** A numerical method used to solve partial differential equations that describe the deformation of materials.
- **Mass-Spring-Damper System:** A more advanced model that includes dampers to simulate energy dissipation and realistic motion.

Challenges in Soft Body Physics

- **Computational Cost:** Soft body simulations can be computationally expensive, especially for large and complex objects.
- **Stability:** Numerical instabilities can lead to unrealistic and unpredictable behavior.
- **Realism:** Achieving realistic deformation and material properties can be challenging.

Techniques for Improving Soft Body Physics

- **Reduced Order Modeling:** Simplifying the model by reducing the number of degrees of freedom.
- **Collision Handling:** Developing efficient and accurate collision detection and response algorithms.
- **Material Modeling:** Simulating the material properties of different substances, such as elasticity, plasticity, and viscosity.
- **GPU Acceleration:** Leveraging the parallel processing power of GPUs to accelerate simulations.

Applications of Soft Body Physics

- **Character Animation:** Creating realistic and expressive character animations.
- **Vehicle Physics:** Simulating the deformation of tires and other vehicle components.
- **Fluid Simulation:** Simulating the behavior of liquids and gases.
- **Cloth Simulation:** Simulating the behavior of clothing and other textiles.

Optimization and Performance

Performance Profiling Tools

Performance profiling tools are invaluable for identifying and addressing performance bottlenecks in graphics applications. By analyzing the performance of different parts of the application, developers can pinpoint areas that need optimization.

Key Performance Metrics:

- **Frame Rate:** The number of frames rendered per second.
- **GPU Utilization:** The percentage of time the GPU is actively working.
- **CPU Utilization:** The percentage of time the CPU is actively working.
- **Memory Usage:** The amount of memory being used by the application.
- **Shader Performance:** The performance of individual shader programs.
- **Draw Calls:** The number of draw calls made to the GPU.

Popular Performance Profiling Tools:

- **NVIDIA Nsight Systems:** A powerful profiling tool that provides detailed information about GPU and CPU performance.
- **AMD Radeon GPU Profiler:** A profiling tool for AMD GPUs that provides insights into shader performance and memory usage.
- **RenderDoc:** A standalone graphics debugger that allows for frame capture, inspection, and analysis.

- **Intel Graphics Performance Analyzer:** A profiling tool for Intel GPUs that provides insights into GPU utilization and performance bottlenecks.

Profiling Techniques:

1. **Frame Profiling:** Analyze the performance of individual frames to identify bottlenecks.
2. **Shader Profiling:** Analyze the performance of individual shader programs to identify inefficient code.
3. **Memory Profiling:** Analyze memory usage to identify memory leaks and inefficient memory allocations.
4. **API Overhead Profiling:** Analyze the overhead of API calls to identify performance bottlenecks.

Performance Optimization Tips:

- **Reduce Draw Calls:** Combine multiple draw calls into fewer, larger draw calls.
- **Optimize Vertex and Index Buffers:** Use vertex and index buffers efficiently to reduce memory usage and improve performance.
- **Optimize Shaders:** Write efficient shaders that minimize instructions and memory accesses.
- **Use Culling Techniques:** Cull objects that are not visible to the camera to reduce the number of objects that need to be rendered.
- **Use Level of Detail (LOD):** Render objects at lower levels of detail when they are far away from the camera.
- **Optimize Texture Usage:** Use texture compression and mipmaps to reduce texture memory usage and improve texture filtering.
- **Use Asynchronous Computations:** Offload computationally expensive tasks to the GPU to improve CPU performance.

Shader Optimization Techniques

Shader optimization is a crucial aspect of performance optimization in graphics applications. By writing efficient shaders, developers can significantly improve the performance of their applications.

Key Shader Optimization Techniques:

1. **Reduce Instructions:**
    - Minimize the number of instructions in a shader.
    - Use built-in functions and hardware instructions whenever possible.
    - Avoid redundant calculations.
2. **Optimize Data Flow:**
    - Minimize the amount of data that needs to be moved between shader stages.
    - Use temporary variables efficiently.
    - Avoid unnecessary data dependencies.
3. **Use Hardware Features:**
    - Leverage hardware features like texture compression, hardware tessellation, and compute shaders.
4. **Unroll Loops:** Unroll small loops to reduce loop overhead.
5. **Use Early Returns:** Return early from shader functions if the result is already known.
6. **Avoid Unnecessary Branches:** Minimize the number of conditional branches in shaders.
7. **Use Built-in Functions:** Utilize built-in functions provided by the graphics API to perform common operations efficiently.

8. **Optimize Texture Access:** Access textures efficiently by using mipmaps and texture compression.
9. **Profile and Analyze:** Use profiling tools to identify performance bottlenecks in shaders.

Shader Optimization Tools:

- **Shader Compiler Optimizations:** Many graphics APIs provide shader compilers that can optimize shaders automatically.
- **Shader Debugger:** Use a shader debugger to visualize shader execution and identify performance issues.

Memory Optimization

Memory optimization is crucial for maintaining high performance and preventing out-of-memory crashes in graphics applications. By efficiently managing memory, developers can improve the overall performance and responsiveness of their applications.

Key Memory Optimization Techniques:

1. **Reduce Texture Memory Usage:**
    - Use texture compression to reduce the size of textures.
    - Use mipmaps to reduce the amount of texture data that needs to be sampled.
    - Use atlas textures to combine multiple small textures into a single larger texture.
2. **Optimize Vertex and Index Buffer Usage:**
    - Use index buffers to reduce the amount of vertex data that needs to be sent to the GPU.
    - Use vertex buffers efficiently to minimize memory usage.

3. **Avoid Redundant Data:**
   - Avoid storing redundant data in multiple places.
   - Use shared resources whenever possible.
4. **Use Memory Pools:** Allocate and deallocate memory from a pool of pre-allocated blocks to reduce memory fragmentation.
5. **Profile Memory Usage:** Use profiling tools to identify memory leaks and memory-intensive operations.
6. **Optimize Resource Management:**
   - Release resources (textures, buffers, shaders) when they are no longer needed.
   - Use resource caching to avoid unnecessary resource loading and unloading.

Memory Optimization Tools:

- **Memory Profilers:** These tools can help identify memory leaks and memory usage patterns.
- **Memory Debugger:** These tools can help debug memory-related issues, such as memory corruption and access violations.

GPU Profiling and Debugging

GPU profiling and debugging are essential tools for identifying and resolving performance issues in graphics applications. By analyzing the performance of GPU operations, developers can optimize their code and improve the overall performance of their applications.

GPU Profiling Tools:

- **NVIDIA Nsight Systems:** A powerful profiling tool that provides detailed information about GPU utilization, shader performance, and memory usage.
- **AMD Radeon GPU Profiler:** A profiling tool for AMD GPUs that provides insights into shader performance and memory usage.
- **RenderDoc:** A standalone graphics debugger that allows for frame capture, inspection, and analysis.
- **Intel Graphics Performance Analyzer:** A profiling tool for Intel GPUs that provides insights into GPU utilization and performance bottlenecks.

GPU Debugging Techniques:

1. **Frame Capture and Inspection:** Capture individual frames and analyze them in detail to identify performance bottlenecks.
2. **Shader Debugging:** Debug shaders to understand their execution flow and identify performance issues.
3. **GPU Timeline Analysis:** Analyze the timeline of GPU operations to identify bottlenecks and inefficiencies.
4. **Memory Profiling:** Analyze memory usage patterns to identify memory leaks and inefficient memory allocations.

Common GPU Performance Issues:

- **Shader Bottlenecks:** Inefficient shaders can significantly impact performance.
- **Memory Bottlenecks:** Inefficient memory usage can lead to performance bottlenecks.
- **Draw Call Overhead:** Too many draw calls can impact performance.
- **State Changes:** Frequent state changes can impact performance.

Tips for GPU Performance Optimization:

- **Reduce Draw Calls:** Combine multiple draw calls into fewer, larger draw calls.
- **Optimize Vertex and Index Buffers:** Use vertex and index buffers efficiently to reduce memory usage and improve performance.
- **Optimize Shaders:** Write efficient shaders that minimize instructions and memory accesses.
- **Use Culling Techniques:** Cull objects that are not visible to the camera to reduce the number of objects that need to be rendered.
- **Use Level of Detail (LOD):** Render objects at lower levels of detail when they are far away from the camera.
- **Optimize Texture Usage:** Use texture compression and mipmaps to reduce texture memory usage and improve texture filtering.

Multi-Threading and Asynchronous Operations

Multi-threading and asynchronous operations are powerful techniques for improving the performance of graphics applications, especially on multi-core systems. By effectively utilizing multiple threads and asynchronous tasks, developers can optimize CPU and GPU usage, leading to smoother and more responsive applications.

Multi-Threading

Multi-threading involves dividing a task into multiple threads, each of which can be executed concurrently on different CPU cores. By distributing the workload across multiple threads, developers can take advantage of modern multi-core processors to improve performance.

Key Considerations for Multi-Threading:

- **Thread Synchronization:** Ensure that threads access shared resources in a synchronized manner to avoid race conditions and data corruption.
- **Thread Safety:** Design code to be thread-safe, especially when multiple threads access shared data.
- **Task Decomposition:** Break down tasks into smaller, independent tasks that can be executed concurrently.
- **Overhead:** Be aware of the overhead associated with creating and managing threads.

Asynchronous Operations

Asynchronous operations allow tasks to be executed independently of the main thread, freeing up the main thread to perform other tasks. This can significantly improve the responsiveness of an application.

Key Considerations for Asynchronous Operations:

- **Task Scheduling:** Use a task scheduler to manage the execution of asynchronous tasks.
- **Callback Functions:** Define callback functions to handle the results of asynchronous operations.
- **Error Handling:** Implement robust error handling mechanisms to deal with potential failures.
- **Synchronization:** Use synchronization primitives like semaphores and mutexes to coordinate the execution of asynchronous tasks.

Common Asynchronous Operations in Graphics:

- **Resource Loading:** Load textures, models, and other assets asynchronously to prevent frame rate drops.
- **GPU Task Submission:** Submit GPU tasks asynchronously to overlap CPU and GPU work.
- **Network Operations:** Perform network operations asynchronously to avoid blocking the main thread.

Case Studies and Projects

Creating a Simple 3D Scene

Creating a simple 3D scene is a great way to start learning Vulkan. This project involves setting up the Vulkan environment, creating a simple triangle, and rendering it to the screen.

Steps Involved:

1. **Set Up the Development Environment:**
   - Install the Vulkan SDK and a suitable C++ compiler (e.g., Clang or GCC).
   - Create a new project directory and set up the necessary build system (e.g., CMake).
2. **Create a Vulkan Instance:**
   - Create a Vulkan instance, which is the entry point to the Vulkan API.
   - Specify the required Vulkan API version and extensions.
3. **Enumerate Physical Devices:**
   - Enumerate the physical devices available on the system (e.g., GPUs).
   - Choose a suitable physical device based on its features and performance.
4. **Create a Logical Device:**
   - Create a logical device, which is a software representation of the physical device.
   - Specify the required device features and queues.
5. **Create Swapchain:**

- Create a swapchain to handle window surface creation and presentation.
- Specify the desired swapchain image format, color space, and presentation mode.

6. **Create Graphics Pipeline:**
   - Create the graphics pipeline, which defines the stages of the rendering pipeline, including vertex and fragment shaders.
   - Specify the vertex input layout, shader stages, and render pass.
7. **Create Vertex and Index Buffers:**
   - Create vertex and index buffers to store the vertex and index data for the triangle.
8. **Record Command Buffers:**
   - Record commands to the command buffer, including setting up the pipeline state, binding vertex and index buffers, and drawing the triangle.
9. **Submit Command Buffers:**
   - Submit the command buffers to the graphics queue for execution.
10. **Present the Image:**
- Present the rendered image to the screen using the swapchain.

Code Example:

C++

```
// ... (Vulkan initialization code)

// Vertex shader
const char* vertexShaderSource = R"(
#version 450
```

```cpp
void main() {
    gl_Position = vec4(0.0, 0.5, 0.0, 1.0);
}
)";

// Fragment shader
const char* fragmentShaderSource = R"(
#version 450

out vec4 FragColor;

void main() {
    FragColor = vec4(1.0, 0.0, 0.0, 1.0); // Red color
}
)";

// ... (Create vertex and index buffers, graphics pipeline, and command buffers)

// Submit command buffer
VkSubmitInfo submitInfo = {};
submitInfo.sType = VK_STRUCTURE_TYPE_SUBMIT_INFO;
submitInfo.commandBufferCount = 1;
submitInfo.pCommandBuffers = &commandBuffer;

vkQueueSubmit(graphicsQueue, 1, &submitInfo, VK_NULL_HANDLE);

// Present the image
VkPresentInfoKHR presentInfo = {};
presentInfo.sType = VK_STRUCTURE_TYPE_PRESENT_INFO_KHR;
presentInfo.waitSemaphoreCount = 1;
```

```
presentInfo.pWaitSemaphores = &imageAvailableSemaphore;
presentInfo.swapchainCount = 1;
presentInfo.pSwapchains = &swapchain;
presentInfo.pImageIndices = &imageIndex;
presentInfo.pImageIndices = &imageIndex;

vkQueuePresentKHR(presentQueue, &presentInfo);
```

Implementing a Real-Time Renderer

A real-time renderer is a core component of many 3D applications, such as games and simulations. It involves rendering a scene at a high frame rate to create a smooth and immersive experience.

Key Components of a Real-Time Renderer:

1. **Scene Graph:** A hierarchical data structure that represents the objects in the scene.
2. **Rendering Pipeline:** The pipeline of stages that processes the scene and produces the final image.
3. **Material System:** A system for defining the appearance of materials, including their color, texture, and lighting properties.
4. **Lighting System:** A system for simulating the interaction of light with objects in the scene.
5. **Camera System:** A system for controlling the camera's position and orientation.

Implementation Steps:

1. **Create a Scene Graph:**

- Define a node structure to represent objects in the scene.
- Create a hierarchical structure of nodes to represent the relationships between objects.

2. **Implement the Rendering Pipeline:**
    - Set up the rendering pipeline stages, including vertex and fragment shaders.
    - Configure the pipeline state, such as rasterization mode, depth testing, and blending.

3. **Create a Material System:**
    - Define material properties, such as albedo, roughness, metallic, and emissive.
    - Implement a shader system to handle material shading.

4. **Implement a Lighting System:**
    - Implement different types of lights, such as directional, point, and spot lights.
    - Calculate lighting for each pixel using techniques like Phong shading or PBR.

5. **Implement a Camera System:**
    - Create a camera class to handle camera position, orientation, and projection.
    - Update the camera's view matrix based on user input or game logic.

Optimization Techniques:

- **Batching:** Combine multiple draw calls into fewer, larger draw calls to reduce CPU and GPU overhead.
- **Culling:** Cull objects that are not visible to the camera.
- **Level of Detail (LOD):** Render objects at lower levels of detail when they are far away from the camera.

- **Texture Compression:** Reduce the size of textures to save memory and improve loading times.
- **Shader Optimization:** Optimize shaders for performance by reducing instructions and memory accesses.

Building a Physically-Based Renderer

A physically-based renderer (PBR) is a rendering technique that simulates the real-world behavior of light interacting with materials. It produces highly realistic and visually appealing graphics.

Core Components of a PBR Renderer:

1. **Material System:**
   - Define material properties like albedo, roughness, metallic, and subsurface scattering.
   - Use texture maps to provide detailed information about material properties.
2. **Lighting System:**
   - Implement various types of lights, including directional, point, and spot lights.
   - Calculate accurate lighting using physically-based lighting models, such as the microfacet BRDF.
3. **Rendering Pipeline:**
   - Configure the rendering pipeline to handle PBR shading.
   - Implement techniques like deferred shading or forward+ rendering to optimize performance.
4. **Post-Processing Effects:**

- Apply post-processing effects like anti-aliasing, bloom, depth of field, and motion blur to enhance the visual quality of the rendered image.

Implementation Steps:

1. **Create a Material System:**
   - Define a material structure to store the material properties.
   - Load texture maps for albedo, roughness, metallic, and normal maps.
2. **Implement a Lighting System:**
   - Calculate the lighting equation for each pixel, taking into account the material properties and light sources.
   - Use techniques like importance sampling to efficiently sample light sources.
3. **Configure the Rendering Pipeline:**
   - Set up the rendering pipeline to handle PBR shading.
   - Use appropriate shader programs to calculate lighting and material properties.
4. **Implement Post-Processing Effects:**
   - Apply post-processing effects to enhance the final image.

Challenges and Considerations:

- **Realism:** Achieving realistic results requires careful tuning of material properties and lighting parameters.
- **Performance:** PBR rendering can be computationally expensive, so optimization techniques are essential.
- **Complexity:** Implementing a full PBR renderer can be complex, requiring a deep understanding of lighting and material theory.

Developing a Game Engine

Core Components of a Game Engine

1. **Graphics Engine:**
   - Handles rendering 3D graphics, including scene graph management, material systems, lighting, and post-processing effects.
   - Utilizes APIs like OpenGL, DirectX, or Vulkan for low-level hardware access.
   - Implements rendering techniques like forward rendering, deferred shading, and physically-based rendering.
2. **Physics Engine:**
   - Simulates the physical behavior of objects in the game world, including rigid body physics, soft body physics, and collision detection.
   - Employs physics engines like PhysX, Bullet, or Box2D.
   - Handles character controllers, vehicle physics, and cloth simulation.
3. **Input System:**
   - Handles input from various devices like keyboards, mice, gamepads, and touchscreens.
   - Provides a unified interface for input handling.
   - Implements input mapping and dead zones.
4. **Sound System:**
   - Handles audio playback, including sound effects and music.
   - Supports various audio formats and spatial audio.
   - Provides tools for sound mixing, filtering, and effects.
5. **Scripting System:**

- Allows game developers to create game logic and behaviors using a scripting language.
- Supports scripting languages like Lua, Python, or C#.
- Provides access to the game engine's APIs and data structures.

6. **Asset Pipeline:**
   - Manages the import, processing, and organization of game assets, such as models, textures, and audio.
   - Supports various asset formats and provides tools for optimizing assets.

7. **Resource Management:**
   - Handles the loading, unloading, and caching of game resources.
   - Implements memory management and resource optimization techniques.

Implementation Challenges

- **Performance Optimization:** Ensuring the game engine can handle complex scenes and effects while maintaining a high frame rate.
- **Cross-Platform Compatibility:** Supporting multiple platforms, such as PC, consoles, and mobile devices.
- **Modularity:** Designing a modular and extensible engine to accommodate different game genres and features.
- **Debugging and Profiling:** Providing tools for debugging and profiling the game engine and games built with it.

Popular Game Engines

- **Unity:** A popular game engine used for a wide range of games, from 2D mobile games to AAA titles.
- **Unreal Engine:** A powerful and feature-rich game engine used for high-end games and real-time simulations.

- **Godot:** An open-source game engine that is easy to learn and use.
- **CryEngine:** A powerful game engine used for realistic and immersive games.

Optimizing a Graphics Application

Optimizing a graphics application involves identifying and addressing performance bottlenecks to improve frame rates, reduce memory usage, and enhance the overall user experience.

Key Optimization Techniques:

1. **Profiling:**
   - Use profiling tools to identify performance bottlenecks.
   - Analyze GPU utilization, CPU utilization, memory usage, and shader performance.
2. **Shader Optimization:**
   - Reduce shader instructions and memory accesses.
   - Use built-in functions and hardware features.
   - Unroll loops and minimize conditional branches.
   - Optimize texture access patterns.
3. **Geometry Optimization:**
   - Reduce the number of polygons in the scene.
   - Use level of detail (LOD) techniques to reduce the complexity of distant objects.
   - Optimize vertex and index buffers.
4. **Draw Call Optimization:**
   - Combine multiple draw calls into fewer, larger draw calls.

- Use instancing to render multiple objects with the same geometry and material.
5. **Texture Optimization:**
    - Use texture compression to reduce texture file sizes.
    - Use mipmaps to reduce texture filtering costs.
    - Use texture atlases to combine multiple textures into a single texture.
6. **Material Optimization:**
    - Reduce the number of material instances.
    - Use material blending and alpha testing to reduce the number of draw calls.
7. **Lighting Optimization:**
    - Use light culling to eliminate unnecessary light calculations.
    - Use lightmaps and shadow maps to reduce the number of dynamic light calculations.
8. **Post-Processing Optimization:**
    - Optimize post-processing effects, such as anti-aliasing and motion blur.
    - Use hardware-accelerated post-processing techniques.

Common Performance Bottlenecks:

- **GPU Bottlenecks:**
    - Limited GPU memory bandwidth.
    - Inefficient shader code.
    - Too many draw calls.
- **CPU Bottlenecks:**
    - Inefficient CPU code.
    - Excessive CPU-GPU synchronization.
- **Memory Bottlenecks:**
    - Excessive memory usage.
    - Inefficient memory allocation and deallocation.

Appendix

Vulkan API Reference

The Vulkan API Reference is a comprehensive documentation resource that provides detailed information about the Vulkan API functions, structures, and constants. It is essential for developers to consult the official API reference when working with Vulkan.

Key Components of the Vulkan API Reference:

1. **Core API:**
   - Defines the core functions and structures for creating Vulkan instances, devices, and pipelines.
   - Covers topics such as memory management, command buffers, synchronization, and rendering pipelines.
2. **Instance Extensions:**
   - Extend the functionality of the Vulkan instance, such as surface creation, window system integration, and debugging.
3. **Device Extensions:**
   - Extend the functionality of a physical device, such as support for specific shader features, advanced rendering techniques, and device-specific capabilities.

Using the Vulkan API Reference:

1. **Search Functionality:** Use the search function to quickly find specific functions, structures, or concepts.

2. **Function and Structure Documentation:** Each function and structure is documented with detailed descriptions, parameters, and return values.
3. **Code Examples:** Many functions and structures are accompanied by code examples to illustrate their usage.
4. **Related Topics:** Links to related topics are provided to help you navigate the documentation.

Tips for Effective Use:

1. **Start with the Basics:** Begin by understanding the core concepts of Vulkan, such as logical and physical devices, queues, and memory management.
2. **Consult the API Reference Regularly:** Refer to the API reference whenever you need specific information about a function or structure.
3. **Experiment and Learn:** Experiment with different Vulkan features and techniques to gain practical experience.
4. **Leverage Community Resources:** Participate in online forums and communities to learn from other developers and get help with specific problems.

Troubleshooting Tips

When working with Vulkan, it's inevitable to encounter issues and errors. Here are some tips to help you troubleshoot and debug your Vulkan applications:

Common Issues and Solutions

1. **Validation Layers:**

- Enable the validation layers to catch common errors and warnings.
- Pay attention to the validation layer messages and warnings.
- Fix the underlying issues identified by the validation layers.

2. **Memory Leaks:**
    - Use memory profiling tools to identify memory leaks.
    - Ensure that all allocated resources are properly freed.
    - Use smart pointers or reference counting to manage memory automatically.

3. **Incorrect Synchronization:**
    - Ensure that synchronization primitives are used correctly to avoid race conditions and deadlocks.
    - Use fences and semaphores to coordinate the execution of commands.

4. **Shader Compilation Errors:**
    - Check for syntax errors and semantic errors in your shader code.
    - Use a shader debugger to step through the shader code and identify issues.
    - Verify that the shader code is compatible with the target GPU.

5. **Rendering Issues:**
    - Check the pipeline state, shader code, and vertex/index buffer data.
    - Use a graphics debugger to visualize the rendering pipeline and identify issues.
    - Ensure that the depth buffer and stencil buffer are configured correctly.

Debugging Tools

- **Vulkan SDK:**
  - Includes validation layers and debugging tools.
  - Provides detailed information about the Vulkan API and its implementation.
- **RenderDoc:**
  - A powerful graphics debugging tool that allows you to capture frames, inspect the rendering pipeline, and analyze performance metrics.
- **GPU Profilers:**
  - Analyze GPU performance and identify bottlenecks.
  - Provide insights into shader performance, memory usage, and pipeline stalls.

Best Practices

- **Clear and Concise Code:** Write clear and concise code to make it easier to understand and debug.
- **Modular Design:** Break down your code into smaller, modular functions to improve readability and maintainability.
- **Thorough Testing:** Test your application on different hardware configurations and operating systems.
- **Continuous Learning:** Stay up-to-date with the latest Vulkan features and best practices.

Common Pitfalls and Solutions

When working with Vulkan, it's easy to encounter common pitfalls that can lead to unexpected behavior or performance issues. Here are some of the most common pitfalls and their solutions:

Common Pitfalls

1. **Incorrect Synchronization:**
     - **Issue:** Incorrectly using synchronization primitives, such as semaphores and fences, can lead to race conditions and undefined behavior.
     - **Solution:** Carefully plan the synchronization of tasks, especially when dealing with multiple threads or asynchronous operations. Use the appropriate synchronization primitives and ensure that they are used correctly.
2. **Memory Leaks:**
     - **Issue:** Failing to release memory resources can lead to memory leaks, which can degrade performance and cause crashes.
     - **Solution:** Use reference counting or smart pointers to manage memory automatically. Ensure that all resources are properly freed when they are no longer needed.
3. **Incorrect Pipeline State:**
     - **Issue:** Incorrectly configuring the pipeline state, such as blending, depth testing, or rasterization modes, can lead to unexpected rendering results.
     - **Solution:** Carefully review the pipeline state configuration and ensure that it is correct for the desired rendering effect.
4. **Shader Compilation Errors:**
     - **Issue:** Syntax errors, semantic errors, or unsupported language features can cause shader compilation to fail.
     - **Solution:** Use a shader compiler to identify and fix errors. Check the shader logs for detailed error messages.

5. **Performance Bottlenecks:**
    - **Issue:** Inefficient algorithms, excessive draw calls, or poorly optimized shaders can lead to performance bottlenecks.
    - **Solution:** Use profiling tools to identify performance bottlenecks. Optimize shaders, reduce draw calls, and use efficient algorithms.

Solutions and Best Practices

- **Use Validation Layers:** Enable the validation layers to catch common errors and warnings.
- **Learn from the Vulkan Documentation:** Refer to the official Vulkan documentation for detailed information and best practices.
- **Use Debugging Tools:** Use tools like RenderDoc and GPU profilers to analyze and debug your application.
- **Optimize Your Code:** Write efficient code, minimize memory usage, and optimize shader performance.
- **Test Thoroughly:** Test your application on different hardware configurations and operating systems.
- **Learn from the Community:** Participate in online forums and communities to learn from other developers and get help with specific problems.

By understanding and avoiding these common pitfalls, you can create high-performance and visually stunning Vulkan applications.

www.ingramcontent.com/pod-product-compliance
Lightning Source LLC
Chambersburg PA
CBHW062118220526
45471CB00010B/3786